INVESTING + DESTINATION
MATSON MONEY WEST

Investing isn't just about the result, it's also about the journey. We hope you'll enjoy your time with us at Matson Money West and your adventure in beautiful Arizona.

AN INVESTING DESTINATION

Join the Matson Money team on an investing adventure like you've never experienced before… at the Matson Money West Facilities in Scottsdale, Arizona.

Traditionally, investing has been relegated to formal boardrooms and stuffy offices. At Matson Money, we believe that investing can be both powerfully inspiring and dare we say it – fun. You are invited to participate in a unique event that has the potential to change the way you view investing, retirement, and your financial future in an environment designed to empower you to take action.

With an independent financial adviser as your guide, you will be our honored guest at our 50,000 square foot facility created with your comfort, education and experience in mind. We will deliver two days of compelling investment and economic education that is relevant to your life and personal circumstances. Our goal is to leave you feeling enabled and motivated to create the financial experience you've always wanted.

When your experience at Matson Money is complete, we hope you take an opportunity to enjoy the amazing opportunities that Arizona has to offer. Scottsdale is, in itself, an amazing destination. Boasting beautiful weather year-round, first class dining, upscale resorts, magnificent hiking trails, vast water parks, world renowned golf, thrilling sporting events, and more. There's no doubt you will have a wonderful time on your visit to Scottsdale.

WORLD CLASS RESORTS

Scottsdale is home to over twenty luxury resorts, giving you plenty of options for visiting in style. Whether your focus is on family fun or relaxing in the serene beauty of this mountain-filled wonderland, there's a resort that will fit your needs. Matson Money has worked to get you discounts at some of the most lavish hotels in Scottsdale.

Westin Kierland (Starwood)

The Westin Kierland is closely located to Scottsdale's finest dining, shopping, and more. With luxurious amenities, beautiful pools, and an amazing spa, you're sure to have a great time staying at this hotel.

Four Seasons

Westin Kierland

Four Seasons

This extravagant retreat is nestled into the foothills of Pinnacle Peak Mountain, surrounded by beautiful views and world class dining, golf, and recreation. This resort offers the ultimate pampering at their on-site spa, incomparable dining options, family activities, stargazing tours, and world-class amenities.

Fairmont Princess

The Fairmont Princess is a AAA Five Diamond Resort in the center of Scottsdale. This resort is home to four top-ranked Arizona restaurants, innovative spa and fitness facilities, six sparkling pools, including the all-new Sunset Beach, and two newly renovated 18-hole championship golf courses. This highly acclaimed Scottsdale resort is truly an experience like no other. Boasting both splash pools and larger pools for family fun, as well as serene desert landscape, endless holiday events and children's activities. This resort has it all.

Fairmont Princess

Hilton Garden Inn

Find everything you need for work and relaxation in this renovated Scottsdale hotel. Equipped with complimentary Wi-Fi and upgraded amenities, this hotel is ideal for families. The hotel features vibrant lounge areas with an outdoor pool, fire pit, whirlpool, and putting green.

Hilton Garden Inn

JW Marriott at Desert Ridge

JW Marriott at Desert Ridge

Situated on 125 acres of the Sonoran Desert, this luxury resort brings a first class experience to its guests. Unwind in style in your own private casita, enjoy exceptional on-site dining, or relax with a round of golf at one of two acclaimed golf courses. Featuring adult-only pools and a world class spa for the ultimate pampering experience, the JW Marriott is an experience you won't soon forget.

Marriott McDowell

Marriott McDowell

With spacious, pet-friendly suites and a terrific location, the Scottsdale Marriott at McDowell Mountains makes hotel living a pleasure. Soak up the sun in extravagant pools and enjoy gourmet cuisine in on-site dining venues.

DINING

Whether you're looking for an intimate meal for two, an extravagant spread for a large group, or a casual venue for the whole family—you'll find the perfect restaurant here in Scottsdale. With first-class seafood and steakhouses as well as down-home country cooking joints, Scottsdale is full of gourmet cuisine for everyone. Boasting no less than 21 restaurants that have been nationally featured on Food Network's *Diners, Drive-Ins and Dives*, the Scottsdale and Phoenix area is bursting with scrumptious options you won't be able to get enough of.

Mastro's

Mastro's Steakhouse – North Scottsdale
Mastro's City Hall Steakhouse – Scottsdale
Mastro's Ocean Club – Scottsdale

These upscale, sophisticated restaurants offer a large selection of steak, seafood, and incredible side dishes. No matter which location you visit, make sure to try their Signature Warm Butter Cake.

Fat Ox

An open and sleek Italian spot offering exquisite housemade pastas and roasted meats, boasting a global wine list. You can't go wrong with their garganelli pasta and homemade gelato.

Olive and Ivy

The Mission (Kierland)

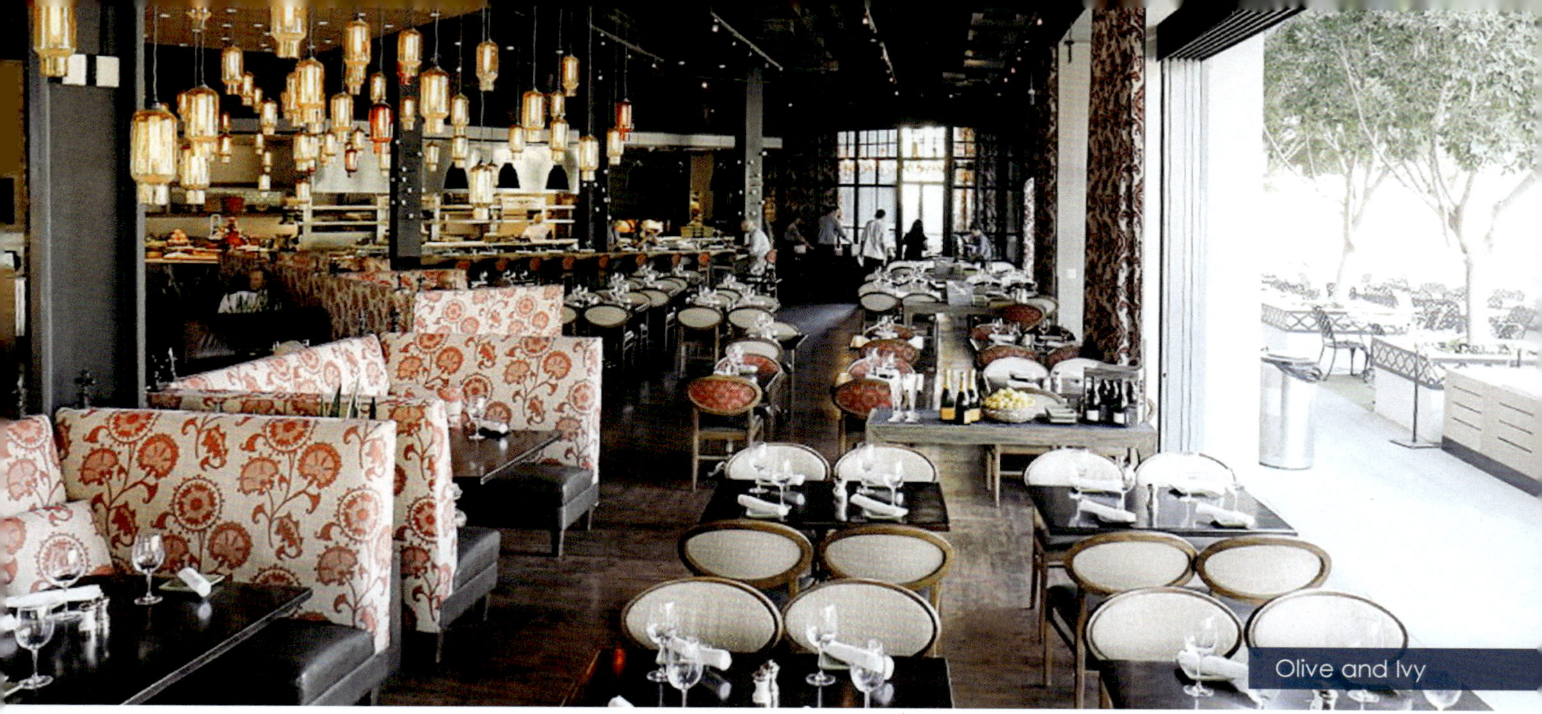

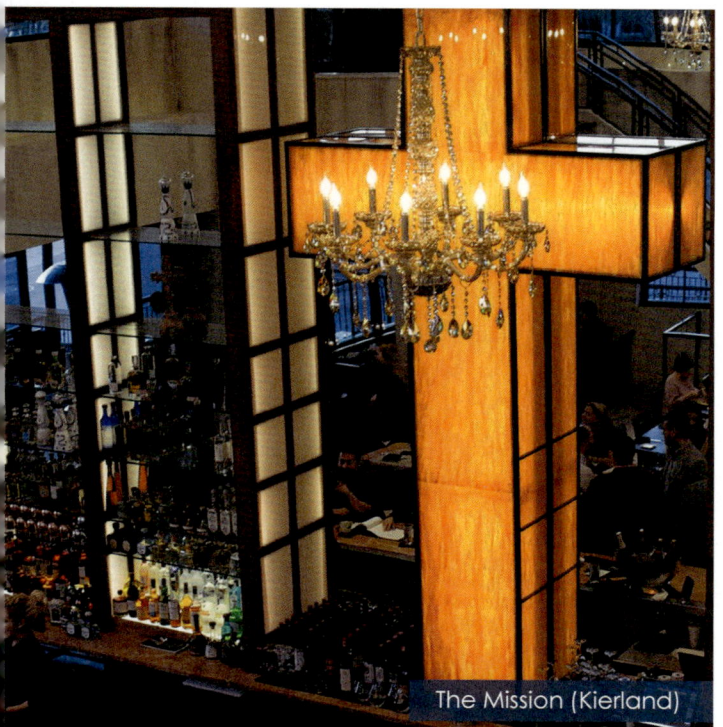

Olive and Ivy

Reminiscent of the French Riviera, serving Californian-Mediterranean fare, Olive and Ivy provides a space that is inviting and relaxing as well as grand and sophisticated. Their beautiful outdoor seating is an experience you don't want to miss.

The Mission

The Mission – Old Town

The Mission – Kierland

This modern Latin joint offers homemade tortillas and salsas that are made fresh daily. The restaurant suits a variety of moods, offering outdoor seating with a view as well as intimate indoor areas, and a lively community table.

HIT THE LINKS

With an average of 330 days of sunshine per year, it is always a good day to hit the course in Scottsdale. The Phoenix area boasts more than 200 courses with unique and dramatic holes set in the desert landscape. Hosting annual PGA, LPGA, and Champions Tour events, there is something for everyone who enjoys the game.

The Phoenician Golf Club

The Phoenician has been ranked among the "Top 75 Golf Resorts in America" by Golf Digest. The Phoenician's three diverse nine-hole courses create 18-hole combinations for a challenging and fun experience in the beautiful scenery of the Scottsdale Mountains.

Tournament Players Club (TPC) Scottsdale

TPC Scottsdale

TPC Scottsdale Champions Course

This PGA-tour approved course is your destination for some intense golfing. Catering to larger groups, this venue is a blast for all and boasts golf shops, dining, and even luxury suites.

Grayhawk Golf Club

The Westin Kierland Golf Club
Honored as one of the "Top 10 Public Courses in Phoenix/Scottsdale" by Golf Advisor. This leading resort course of Arizona has three championship-style nines – each with its own flavor and strategy.

Wildfire Golf Club
Wildfire Golf Club is situated in the rugged Sonoran Desert of Northeast Phoenix, and features two picturesque 18-hole championship courses designed golf greatest legends Arnold Palmer and Nick Faldo.

Grayhawk Golf Club
This challenging yet rewarding 36-hole course offers two 18-hole options that remain open to everyone – The Raptor Course & Talon Course. Don't miss out on the beautiful views this course offers. We suggest stopping by their restaurant, Isabella's Kitchen, after your game for exquisite pastas and salads.

SHOP TILL YOU DROP

Scottsdale is home to more than 2,500 retailers and malls, including Scottsdale Fashion Square, the Southwest's largest shopping destination. With beautiful weather year-round, the Scottsdale and Phoenix area boasts multiple open-air malls where you can shop in luxury. The Scottsdale Quarter and Kierland Commons offer a retail experience like no other with upscale shops and dining in a beautiful outdoor setting.

Kierland Commons

Kierland Commons offer an outdoor space full of shopping and dining options in the heart of Scottsdale that is sure to entertain the whole family.

Scottsdale Quarter

The Scottsdale Quarter is one of the largest outdoor shopping and dining hubs in Arizona. A visit to the quarter allows you to shop your favorite stores, enjoy a meal at one of many fine restaurants, and enjoy entertainment for the entire family.

Desert Ridge Marketplace

The Desert Ridge Marketplace District shopping center offers 1.2 million square feet of incredible, outdoor shopping experience boasting splash pads for children, a newly renovated movie theater, and live entertainment in the evenings.

Kierland Commons

Desert Ridge Marketplace

Marshall Way Arts District

Scottsdale Fashion Square Mall

Scottsdale Fashion Square is a vast upscale shopping center featuring over 225 retail stores. It is the largest shopping mall in the American Southwest with nearly 2 million square feet of retail space. You won't want to miss the chance to experience this mall with its luxury brands, exclusive entertainment, and quality service.

Biltmore Fashion Park

Known as the "crown jewel" because of its regal history and unmatched ambiance, Biltmore Fashion Park is an outdoor shopping experience in a park-like setting and serves as home to some of the finest shopping in Arizona.

Marshall Way Arts District

Marshall Way Arts District offers even more shopping options, boasting unique art galleries, western jewelers, and vintage shops reminiscent of old town Scottsdale. No matter what you're shopping for on your visit, you're sure to find it in Scottsdale.

Outlets at Anthem

The outlets at Anthem allow you to shop over 60 brand name stores at large discounts in a family-friendly environment. With train rides and playgrounds for children as well as high end stores and fine dining, there's no doubt the whole family will have fun on a shopping trip at the Anthem Outlets.

NIGHTLIFE

If you adventure into Scottsdale at night, you'll see a city that comes alive with wine bars, night clubs, casinos, and dance clubs. With so many venues and different flavors of nightlife, there's something for everyone.

City Scape Phoenix
Located in downtown Phoenix, this area offers a variety of restaurants, bars and retail shops along with a comedy club and bowling alley.

Rhythm Room
This roots, blues and concert venue offers nationally-acclaimed music acts on a nightly basis.

The Yard/Culinary Dropout
Enjoy playing Ping-Pong or cornhole while sipping on specialty cocktails. This roomy venue offers delicious bar bites and a fun atmosphere - make sure to try their soft pretzels and BBQ pork belly nachos!

Talking Stick Resort

Old Town Scottsdale

Casinos
Casinos are also a large part of the nightlife in Scottsdale, offering a fun night out for groups or couples. With five luxury casinos nearby, there are plenty of options to choose from if you're looking for a night out with lady luck!

Old Town Scottsdale
Old Town Scottsdale boasts nightlife full of handcrafted cocktails, historic western bars, and vintage lounges great for winding down and mingling with new friends.

OUTDOOR ADVENTURE

Arizona is home to some of the most exciting, thrilling, and sensational outdoor adventures in the country. From hiking to biking to ATV tours, water sports, and more, there's always an adventure to go on in Scottsdale! The vast mountain ranges, as well as man-made lakes, make this the perfect spot to go exploring, whether you choose to go on foot, horseback, or hot air balloon. We are sure you'll have a great time!

Hot Air Expeditions

Experience Arizona from a whole new perspective on a hot air balloon ride. These rides boast a view up to 3,000 feet above the desert, and afterwards feel free to enjoy a gourmet breakfast or evening drinks and appetizers. It's not hard to see why Phoenix hot air balloon rides have been a favorite of tourists and native Arizonians for many years.

Hot Air Expeditions

Salt River Tubing & Recreation

Salt River Tubing & Recreation
Go tubing down the Salt River for a fun outdoor Arizona adventure. Remember your water shoes, sunblock and water for this exciting tubing trip!

Lake Life
Visit one of the three most popular lakes that the Arizona Valley has to offer:

- *Lake Saguaro is about 45 minutes East of Matson Money*
- *Bartlett Lake is about 50 minutes North-East of Matson Money*
- *Lake Pleasant is about 45 minute North-West of Matson Money*

Check out each individual website for their water sport rental options.

Lake Saguaro

Arizona Outdoor Fun

Arizona Outdoor Fun

Arizona Outdoor Fun is your complete one-stop shop for all your Arizona outdoor recreational fun. Everything you'd possibly need for outdoor recreation is here including affordable ATV rentals, jet ski rentals, sport quads, motorcycle rentals, and more!

Stellar Adventures

Experience the thrill of navigating through the rugged desert landscape on a H1 Hummer, M1009 Blazer/Jeep, or a guided ATV tour. Offering a unique team building experience for large groups, or simply a day with your family taking on the desert, you're sure to love this high intensity adventure!

Stellar Adventures

Green Zebra Adventures

Get ready to explore 28,000 private acres of the Sonoran Desert in your own specially-designed, military grade, off-road vehicle with an experienced local guide leading the way. This is sure to get your heart racing!

Green Zebra Adventures

Stellar Adventures

Cave Creek Outfitters

Cave Creek Outfitters has something for everyone: guided horseback rides, jeep tours, cowboy cookouts, authentic cowboy games, old west entertainment, wagon rides, corporate events, private parties, and so much more!

Los Cedros

Los Cedros is one of the finest horse training facilities in the world. Available for one-of-a-kind group events as well as horse shows and tours, this venue has many experiences to offer. Get booked today for your personalized event or for a visit with the many horses who call Los Cedros home.

MacDonald's Ranch

MacDonald's Ranch is the premier horseback riding stable in the Valley of the Sun. Located in the tranquil Sonoran Desert, this ranch offers the perfect relaxing desert getaway.

WindWalker Expeditions

WindWalker specializes in private horseback excursions across desert terrain. These exciting, private adventures include river crossings, steep inclines, and narrow canyons.

Windwalker Expeditions

Arizona Outback Adventures

Camelback

Arizona Outback Adventures

If you're looking for an adventure in the mountains, look no further. This bike rental store is conveniently located in North Scottsdale at the foot of the McDowell Mountains, near Frank Lloyd Wright Blvd and the 101 freeway. There is year-round world-class riding right outside our front door!

Hiking

- Gateway Loop
- Pinnacle Peak Park
- Piestwa Peak - Summit Trail
- Sunrise Trail
- Tom's Thumb
- Camelback
  - *Cholla Trailhead*
  - *Echo Canyon Trail*

ACTIVITIES

There's always something exciting to get into when you're in Scottsdale. Whether you're looking for something relaxing, or an activity to get your heart racing- you'll find it here!

Octane Raceway

America's Best Kart Racing! Octane Raceway is the only full time indoor and outdoor Go Kart track in the United States. It features a 1/3 mile track, 45+ mph karts, a bar & grill, billiards, mini-bowling, arcade, and event rooms. You're sure to find something here for the whole family!

Phoenix International Raceway

Phoenix International Raceway is a 1.022 mile low-banked tri-oval race track. The motorsport track opened in 1964 and currently hosts two NASCAR race weekends annually. Get ready for a day of fast cars and fun!

The Penske Auto Museum

The Penske Auto Museum features an impressive collection of cars, trophies, and racing memorabilia chronicling the career of one of the most successful dynasties in all of sports. With replicas of the cars Penske drove to victory in races such as the 1963 Riverside 250, along with trophies and cars that the famed driver actually drove, this museum is a thrill for all!

AZ on the Rocks

This expansive air-conditioned locale is the largest indoor rock-climbing experience in Arizona. Offering a variety of activities including: yoga, fitness classes, and private parties, you're sure to have a great time.

Black Rock Bouldering

Black Rock Bouldering is an indoor gym dedicated to rock-climbing adventures. Bring a group to climb, book the venue for a private event, or simply show up for an unbelievable workout. In addition to 5,000 sq. ft. of climbing walls they have traditional gym equipment including free weights, a fitness area to improve flexibility, body strength, and cardio.

Top Golf

This premier entertainment and event venue gives you the best of both worlds with fun point-scoring golf games in the comfort of a restaurant style venue. Perfect for all skill levels, this family friendly venue also boasts upscale bar food and drinks, great music, and more!

AZ on the Rocks

Top Golf

Desert Botanical Gardens

Desert Botanical Gardens
Located in Papago Park, these gardens offer visitors an opportunity to learn about desert flora and interact with botanical wonders in a fun, family friendly environment.

iFLY
iFLY is the entertainment company that created modern indoor skydiving… make the dream of flight a reality in a safe and reliable environment.

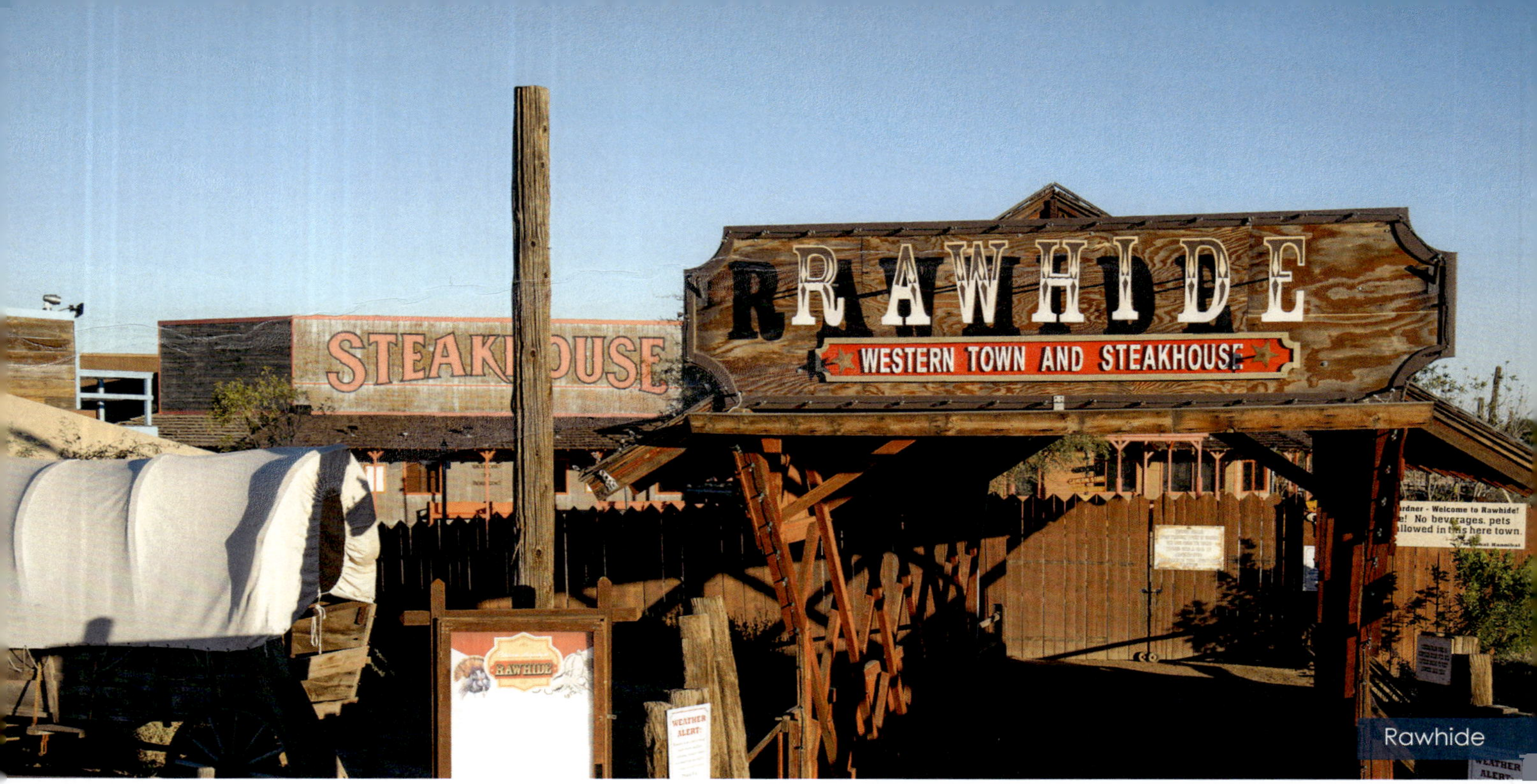

Rawhide

Rawhide

Rawhide is a theme-park eatery in Chandler, AZ. This exciting park offers wagon rides, rock-climbing, bull riding, a shooting gallery, and lots more. You're sure to find fun for the whole family with the near constant holiday and country themed events, along with vast dining opportunities - heavy on the barbecue.

Waste Management Open

The Phoenix Open is a professional golf tournament on the PGA Tour, held in late January/early February at the Tournament Players Club of Scottsdale, Arizona.

Waste Management Open

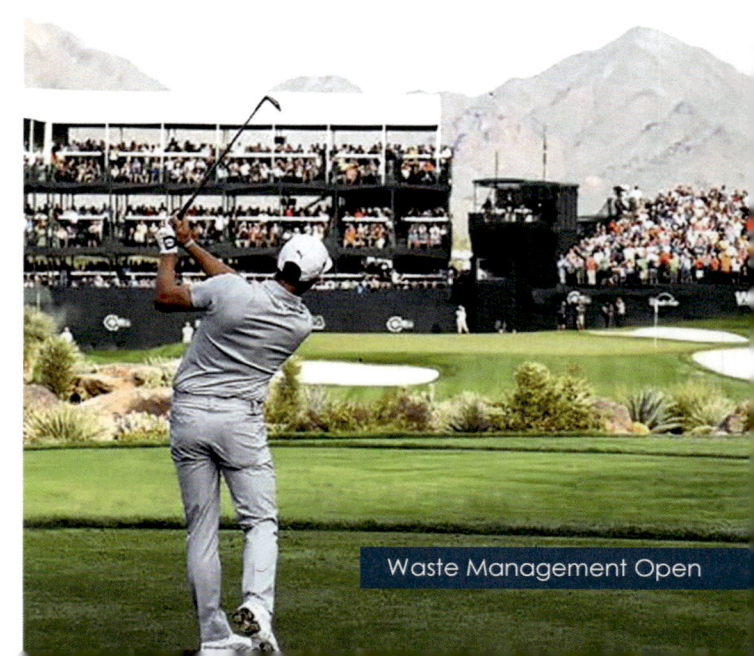

MLB Spring Training

The Cactus League allows you to see 15 teams prepare for the season in a relatively tight radius surrounding the beautiful Valley of the Sun -- Phoenix, Arizona.

Barrett-Jackson Car Show

Usually held in January

The world's greatest classic car auction. This event has some of the most incredible cars in the world and draws thousands of guests each year. This family friendly car show is fun for all ages and you won't want to miss it!

MLB Spring Training

Barrett-Jackson Car Show

SIGHTS

If you're looking to explore even more of Arizona, there are numerous destinations close by with extraordinary landmarks and spirits. Within a few hours are some of the most famous and stunning views in all of the world.

The Grand Canyon

The Grand Canyon is one of the largest attractions in America. This incredible landscape, carved out by the Colorado River, reveals the power of nature and the wonder it can create. The impressive canyon walls glow a variety of colors in the late afternoon sun, and can be enjoyed by travelers of all ages. Whether you're up for a day of hiking or just wanting to catch a glimpse of this marvel, the Grand Canyon won't disappoint. -*About four hours north of Phoenix.*

The Grand Canyon

Sedona

The town of Sedona is situated in a stunning setting surrounded by red rock mountains. There are fabulous views from the main highway running through the town and almost every street corner. With one-of-a-kind coffee shops, hiking trails, and atmosphere, this town is a huge tourist attraction. The area has great hiking and mountain biking, but jeep tours provide an even easier way to get out into the landscape. -*The town of Sedona, about an hour and a half drive north of Phoenix.*

Red Mountains of Sedona

Flagstaff

Flagstaff is nestled in the world's largest Ponderosa Pine Forest and it is at a cool 7,000-foot elevation. Boasting 7 national parks and monuments to visit, and only 80 miles away from the Grand Canyon- you're sure to find adventure in this small town no matter what time of year it is. Favorite warmer weather activities include hiking, mountain biking, disk golf, camping, boating and rock climbing. During the winter months, Flagstaff is host to countless skiers and snowboarders, as well as many families who come to enjoy the snow. *-Flagstaff, about two hours north of Phoenix.*

Flagstaff

Hoover Dam

Hoover Dam is one of the world's great engineering marvels. This massive structure, completed in 1935, crosses the Colorado River, linking Arizona and Nevada. It is 726 feet high and 1,244 f long. Lake Mead, held back by the Hoover Dam, is the largest artificial lake in the United States. It is 110 miles long, and holds the equivalent of two years of flow of the Colorado River. *-The Hoover Dam, about four hours northwest of Phoenix.*

Hoover Dam

Jerome

Once the largest mining town in the west, Jerome's glory days are long gone. This historic treasure is known as "the largest ghost town in America," thanks to the Depression of the 1930's. The town today is alive in a new way, with historic charm abounding in their many Inns, Bed and Breakfasts, restaurants, and music saloons. For a slow-paced, historic, and quaint get away, Jerome is a must-see. *-The town of Jerome, about two hours north of Phoenix.*

Ghost Town of Jerome

SPORTS

When it comes to professional sports teams and events, Arizona is in a whole new league! With baseball, football, soccer, hockey, and more, there's always a fun sporting event to take advantage of. We hope you can get a glimpse of the Arizona Cardinals, Phoenix Suns, Arizona Diamondbacks, Arizona Coyotes, Arizona Rattlers, Phoenix Rising FC, or the Phoenix Mercury while you're in town and get a chance to visit one of the state-of-the-art sports facilities these teams call home!

If you're interested in playing yourself, there are tons of sporting adventures for individuals or whole families! From little league baseball fields to world-famous golf courses, there are amenities for all age levels to get active and enjoy a little sporting of their own!

Phoenix Suns

Cardinals Football Stadium

Arizona Diamondbacks

Arizona Coyotes

FAMILY

We encourage guests to bring their families to Arizona for the chance to make once-in-a-lifetime memories together. There are so many activities and adventures to enjoy in this sunny sanctuary. For younger guests we recommend taking advantage of the large amount of kid-friendly attractions in Arizona. There are hundreds of parks, zoos, wildlife adventures, and waterparks to excite and thrill the whole family.

LegoLand Arizona
LegoLand Arizona offers exciting rides, 4-D movies, and the chance to build unique creations for younger children. -*Arizona Mills Mall in Tempe.*

Sea Life Arizona
Sea Life Arizona is an interactive aquarium that contains thousands of aquatic creatures, plus interactive touch pools and a 360° ocean tunnel and spans over 26,000 square feet. -*Arizona Mills Mall in Tempe.*

Butterfly Wonderland

Butterfly Wonderland

Butterfly Wonderland is the largest indoor butterfly pavilion in America, and gives you an up close and personal experience with these beautiful creatures. Family friendly and located near other entertainment spots, you won't want to miss out!

OdySea Aquarium

Be sure you don't miss the new and incredible OdySea aquarium! This 200,000 square foot aquarium holds more than 2 million gallons of water and is home to over 10,000 animals! This new facility allows you to explore a whole new underwater world with options to get up close and personal with some of the animals, check out engineering marvels as you navigate through the tunnels and tanks, and play with the creatures like never before in their state-of-the-art touch pools!

OdySea Aquarium

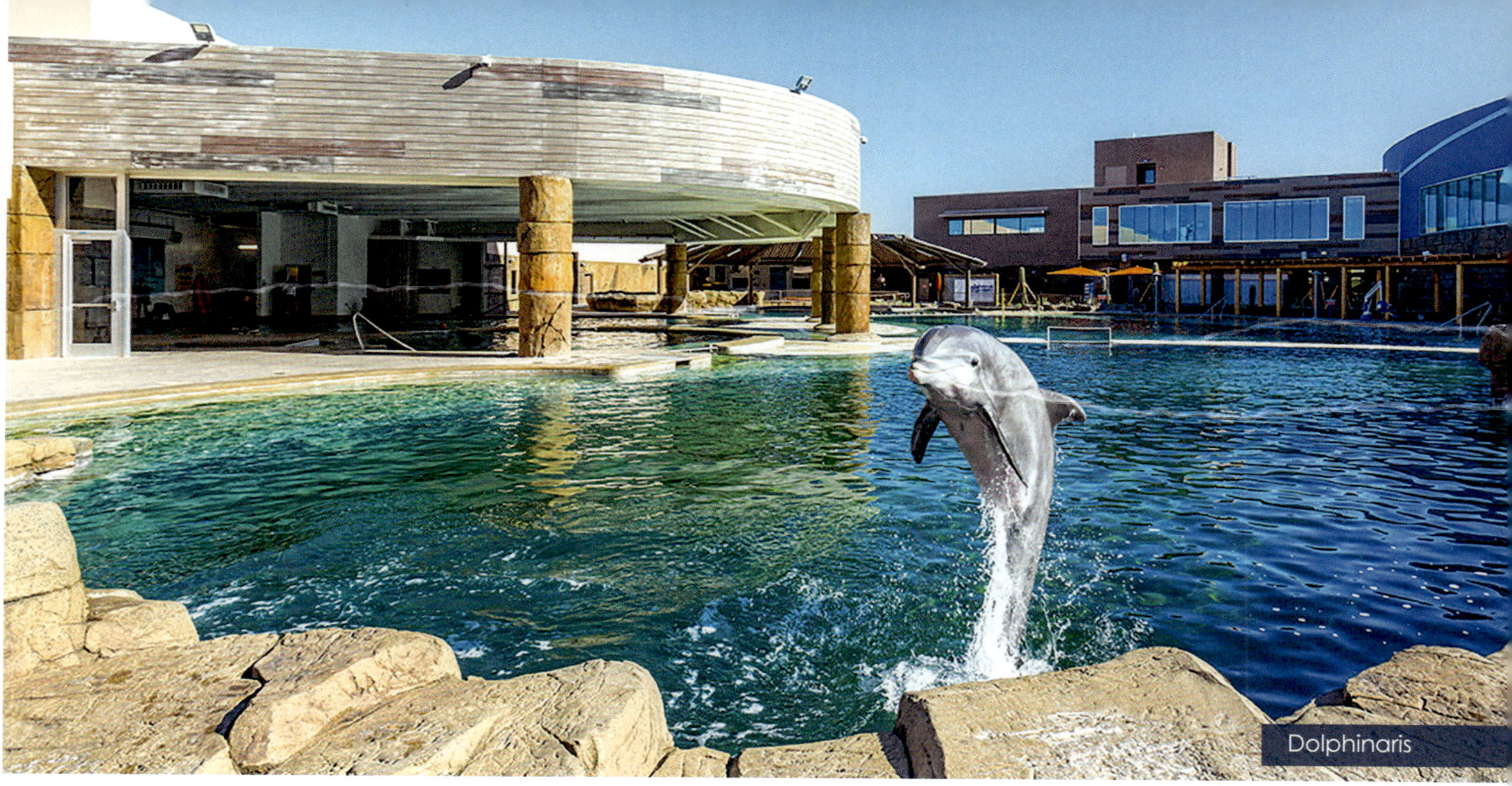

Dolphinaris

Phoenix Zoo

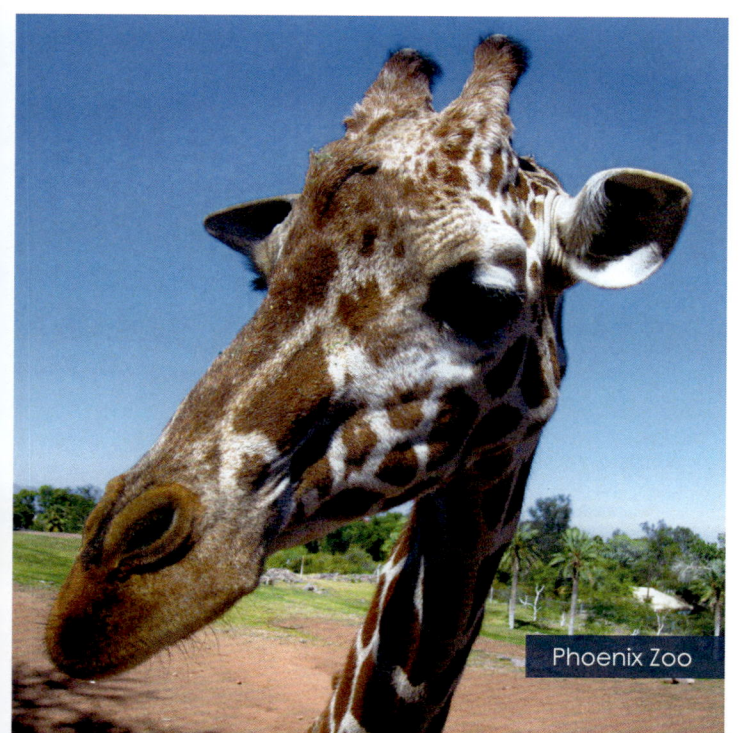

Dolphinaris Arizona

Visitors are encouraged to swim with dolphins in this his modern marine habitat offering viewing tanks & open-air pools.

Phoenix Zoo

The non-profit Phoenix Zoo is home to more than 1,400 animals including more than 30 different endangered or threatened species from around the world. Enjoy a day riding the carousel, devouring ice cream treats, and taking in the rare wildlife in this beautiful zoo.

Wet n' Wild Waterpark

The largest waterpark in Phoenix, with slides and water fun for all ages! Wet n' Wild offers plenty of fun for kids and adults alike, as well as dive in movies and holiday events!

Big Surf

McCormick Ranch Train Park

Wet n' Wild Waterpark

Big Surf
Big Surf is a waterpark located in Tempe, Arizona, boasting the United State's first wave pool.

McCormick Ranch Train Park
This 30-acre park, located in the heart of Scottsdale, Arizona, is the most unique park of its kind in the country. Take a ride on the Paradise & Pacific Railroad and the 1950-vintage carousel. Visit a variety of shops and museums, play on one-of-a-kind playgrounds, or enjoy ice cream with the kids!

CULTURE

A highlight of any visit to Greater Phoenix is the area's rich arts-and-culture environment. Performances at a multitude of theaters, concert halls, and cultural centers are constant attractions, while art and history lovers can flock to a diverse group of fascinating museums.

Frank Lloyd Wright's Taliesin West

Frank Lloyd Wright's Taliesin West, Scottsdale's only National Historic Landmark, offers tours of Wright's winter home and grounds. Tours weave through Wright's desert masterpiece visiting the gracious Garden Room, the Cabaret, and the Pavilion where the master entertained. Linked by provocative terraces, gardens, and walkways, guides lead guests through multiple structures designed by Wright while outlining the colorful history of Taliesin West and its creator.

The Musical Instrument Museum

In just six short years since opening, the Musical Instrument Museum (MIM) has been recognized as one of the top 20 museums in the United States and is rated the #1 attraction in Phoenix by TripAdvisor reviewers. MIM provides a fun, one-of-a-kind experience to be enjoyed by guests of all ages.

The Musical Instrument Museum

Frank Lloyd Wright's Taliesin West

Heard Museum

Heard Museum

The Heard Museum is an Art and Native Cultures Museum featuring collections of art, libraries, and archives, and typically presenting exhibits on things such as native cultures or landscapes of the past. Their focus is on educating visitors and promoting greater public understanding of the arts, heritage, and life ways of the indigenous peoples of the Americas.

Western Spirit

Phoenix Art Museum

Arizona Science Center

Western Spirit: Scottsdale's Museum of the West

Located in Old Town Scottsdale this Western Spirit Museum opened in January of 2015 and boldly immerses its guests in the unique story of the Greater Western region.

Phoenix Art Museum

This Museum provides an extensive collection of acclaimed art spanning from the Renaissance to the present. This gallery holds pieces from more than 19,000 objects of modern and contemporary art, fashion design, and photography.

Children's Museum of Phoenix

Kids are sure to love this expansive museum with 300-plus interactive play areas, interactive experiences, musical activities, and more designed for babies to kids up to age 10.

Arizona Science Center

The Science Center engages curious minds through hands-on interaction with science. Featuring permanent exhibits as well as limited-time rotating scientific exploration opportunities, the Science Center speaks to all ages.

Matson Money Concierge

CONCIERGE

Make sure your trip to Matson Money West and Scottsdale is everything you imagined with a little help from our Concierge team. They are here to assist you with dinner recommendations and reservations, hotel recommendations, golf outings, and any recreational activities.

Connect with Concierge:

concierge@matsonmoney.com
513.204.8000

Made in the USA
Columbia, SC
19 November 2018